ENIGMA

Let these rhapsodies / sew up / the

AND LIGHT
rhetoric of high and low

AHSAHTA PRESS
BOISE, **IDAHO**

2012

THE NEW **SERIES**

#47

ENIGMA AND LIGHT

DAVID MUTSCHLECNER

Ahsahta Press, Boise State University, Boise, Idaho 83725-1525
http://ahsahtapress.boisestate.edu
http://ahsahtapress.boisestate.edu/books/mutschlecner3/mutschlecner3.htm
Cover design by Quemadura
Book design by Janet Holmes
Printed in Canada

LIBRARY OF CONGRESS CATALOGING-IN-PUBLICATION DATA

Mutschlecner, David.
Enigma and light / David Mutschlecner.
p. cm. -- (The new series ; no. 47)
ISBN 978-1-934103-28-9 (pbk. : alk. paper) — ISBN 1-934103-28-4 (pbk. : alk. paper)
I. Title.
PS3563.U855E55 2012
811'.54--DC23
2011043608

ACKNOWLEDGMENTS

Thank you to Paul Hoover of *New American Writing* for publishing "Herman Melville / Martin Puryear," "Martin Heidegger / Ezra Pound," and "Oscar Muñoz / Emmanuel Levinas."

FOR MY **FAMILY**

CONTENTS

Gertrude Stein / Agnes Martin   1

Robert Ryman / Nicholas of Cusa   8

Herman Melville / Martin Puryear   16

Charles Burchfield / John Henry Newman   20

The Gee's Bend Quilters / The Museum of Modern Art   27

Georges Rouault / Robert Motherwell   31

Martin Heidegger / Ezra Pound   36

Oscar Muñoz / Emmanuel Levinas   40

Karl Rahner / The Dusky Seaside Sparrow   44

Thomas Aquinas / Emily Dickinson   52

Joan Mitchell / Charles Olson   53

Robert Duncan / Dante Alighieri   57

Francis / Clare   62

Marc Chagall / Alexis Palmaffy   66

Mother / Son   74

Saint Faustina / Karol Wojtyla   78

Enigma and Light in Every Relation I   82

Enigma and Light in Every Relation II   91

Notes   97

GERTRUDE STEIN / AGNES MARTIN

1

"Loving repeating is one way of being;
    this is now a description of such feeling."

Milk River: hours and hours, days of lines.
    Hundreds of horizontal
        parallels in pale

red on off white as if all
    milk were threaded secretly with blood,
        innocent sustenance
        with sacrifice.

As I write I rock
    back and forth—something coming down
        this line toward me.

2

A field suffuse with yellow snake weed or purple aster.
    A single flower.
        Flower by flower . . .

The scientist finds elegance in pattern
    and in irruptions of pattern
        that are themselves patterned past all understanding;

and the mathematician in law that passes
    beyond mortal making. The Psalmist
        loves the law and praises its earthly echoes.

A man and a woman love each other through habit,
    love and hate one another repeated
        across their commingled lifetimes.

3

"Always
    from the beginning there was to me all
    living as repeating." And repeating leading
        into quiet's quotidian.

But what does this lined
    litany
        sing of its source,

a source I seem
    to have lost in labor,

swaying over the timed
    objects of the museless
        marketplace,

stacked and depleted
    stacked and depleted
        across the decades.

Martin makes grids
    to graph
        nothing—

a grid
    plunging
        into itself—

myriad cells for light under light.
    line upon finite line—signate matter, snares
        for light's namesake.

If this indeed is the direction
    then one cannot say
        one and one and one and one

enough times. "Some then have always growing in them
    more and more loving feeling for repeating
        the whole of them."

How do you get to the whole?
    "Humility,
        the beautiful daughter."

4

Along the stream of lights are nodal points,
    each a "radiant gist,"
        a "patterned event"

as Pound once called the image.
    One and one and one
        come down the line to meet *this* one.

Martin's marks are Stein's
    word stipplings,
        both inter-patterning one another

as they could not
    without the clear delineation—
        each word girded by the grid.

Gray Stone: thousands of precise
    short blue vertical strokes
        small as fingerprints—

a sea of personality
    holding the trace

        of each
        brush
        stroke

over a gold leaf grid—
    a sea whose singularity
        dissolves in a blown leaf shimmer.

5

"There was a long time then when there was nothing in me using
    the bottom loving repeating being that now leads me to knowing."
        Martin discovered her art when she discovered

the innocence of the grid as the innocence
    of trees—
        Mondrian's limbs repeating as divine geometry.

After work I see the shadow of the Venetian blinds
    patterned across the corner of my room,
        steeped in stillness as in beauty.

In every repetition
    let meaning bless measure
        and measure / meaning.

ROBERT RYMAN / NICHOLAS OF CUSA

A semicolon right at the center
of an empty page—a fulcrum
balancing what?

The mind consigned to quiet
yet swaying on an elegant
silver hook.

The poem of a semicolon alone
is a joke to the loquacious
novelist, but what great

leviathan are we both
trying to bate? Is the world
and its idea

pinned together
by something so fragile,
wavering there in space?

Am I close to the point
wavering there?
Perhaps

the semicolon hangs
as a brooch on the breast
of day and night

—a moon with a curved
wisp of cloud
below it.

If the blank page were simply bracketed
at upper left and lower right,
it wouldn't be

as interesting a poem.
(I hear Parmenides
gruffly disagree;

I hear Heraclitus assent,
though he mostly
complains of cold

and asks whoever is the poet
to make a fire
—to make

the writing luminous and haloed
and yet darkly intractable
as if

burned in.) Be careful
about the blank slate
because it is never really blank—

the beginning not inchoate,
but full of rising proclivities
swept out in registers of fire,

a fundament whose filament
is subtle beyond idea.
Beyond the dreamed

beginning, the breathed
beginning, the ignition
of primordial equation.

Four bolts at the center
of a white square
hold the painting

to the wall—
at once the fasteners
and fixers of vision

which expands
from the bright
metal points

to the four corners
of the panel
done purely

in white. This
is Robert Ryman's
Expander. The inverse

of a night sky where
the moon might
expand sight to the dark edges

—so it is a kind of universe
with something at the center:
a steely act

anchoring everything
while pushing everything
to its limit; so

ousia is *telos*
from the start.
And the white:

is it a covering
or a first offering?
A pure potency

or some kind
of primordial act?
Be careful

of the *tabula rasa,*
because there is already
a world there

just on the other side—
this note pinned to the winter
coat of the school-bound child.

The apophatic flower blooms
in the dead of winter,
after Christmas

when the sweets have all been eaten,
when the temperature drops
to zero, and the moon

is crystalline, a white flower buried
in a sky of black ice.
But the apophatic

flower is not the moon,
though the moon
may shine upon it:

flares in frozen glass.
Nor can its petals be seen.
The apophatic flower is our mortal cloak

and crown: hooded
hope in a moment's
unnotice

which is most of our lives.
The nothing / not nothing,
a flood of otherness in faith,

but often through abandoned space.
I "incomprehensibly understand"
wrote Nicholas of Cusa on the cusp

of modernism, circa 1450;
and I understand what he means
I think. Two halves of the page,

now with an eye between.
One side: apophatic,
the other: cataphatic,

white paper,
dark writing. Only together
are they a beginning—

not knowing become in humbleness
a glowing node in the knowing.
The semicolon

balanced at the center of the sky,
the balance point itself as affirmation:
the nothing / not nothing,

the Dickinsonian dash,
the white cracks in the black
pavement on the first

snowy day of winter—
some sort of inversion or conversion
where *yes* wells in the willed silence.

HERMAN MELVILLE / MARTIN PURYEAR

The plowed parking lot
has its massed harvest
by December's end—
a white hump, cornered

by commerce, grayed
by February. Its nine
feet seem
to last and last,

more sculptured stone than snow.
Finally, March rain
wears the pocked surface away.
No one sees it melt,

it only fades,
revealing in layers
the debris of December—
here a wet ribbon, there a sodden string

tangled in the effluence of a cold
sunken hump.
Our allowance of white whale
under the black wet pavement.

We stand in the parking lot's cold
and talk about the man who was found
frozen to death
curled on the stoop

of the realtor's office.
The bower of his own perfect
curving ribs (a kind of slow
drowning) a wrestling breath . . .

but what do I know
of freezing to death? "In nature,"
Duncan wrote,
"the furies stir."

The coffin-canoe that Queequeg
rested in,
that was a carving by Martin Puryear;
and the lighted pole stuck in the spout hole

and the rope ladders in the rigging,
climbed to the point
where they are rungless spires—
these are his.

To seek to kill the furies
is to be a hooked
fury, a curved
inverted sharpness.

Better to carve waves in grieving space.
Carve them in granite on a red wood floor.
Carve them in soapstone on marble.
Make one of clunky crosshatch

and call it *Thicket*,
an out-of-business wave.
Weave one in wicker and call it *Bower*—
a basket to make it.

Carve them in white pine on ebony. Carve prayers
—curved   disclosures
from the hidden hub, heliotropic wheels,
rudders imagined

beneath the floor.
The mind is for the world,
poured out, broken,
like the king's spikenard at a christening.

I might ask Puryear
to carve for Pip a fragrant
cedar corpus on a white pine cross
to hold in his arms like Queequeg's Yojo,

        to hold in my arms when I sleep.

CHARLES BURCHFIELD / JOHN HENRY NEWMAN

We
keep on
adding sides
to the equation

conflating its complexion
with everything under the sun
until it is in fact everything under the sun

and we are walking there,
our pregnant emotions
having given birth to a world.

We have passed through
a doorframe made
of bent tree boughs—

no door, no walls—
and have entered into where
we are already

except now the landscape
seems as peripatetic
as any of us might be—

thought rolls and turns and
catches the crest-
light epiphany

even as the shadow of the working
class valley
remains ashen.

In the postage stamp
back yard, under the shabby
shrubbery,

(even in my
day laborer's
cornered mind

there is a hollow
where my brother
plays the cello)

a Charles Burchfield opening.
It is no colder outside than in—
the world a reversible

fabric—it keeps on going,
what ever it is.
We are first

apprehensive
about seeing little signs
of ourselves in everything,

but it isn't long
before we are revelers
in anthropomorphism—

things just a step away
from us, hiding in their trans-
seasonal dew.

"Our most natural mode of reasoning is
not from proposition to proposition,
but from thing to thing,

from whole to whole."
—that is strong man John
Henry Newman

whose steel-driven
pragmatism
sparks grace.

Raven shadow soars
over the road,
then lifts

with the raven to the tree
where it breaks
into shadow-feathers,

a flitting multiplicity
equated with the leaves,
become one

undulation of black
and green,
while the raven

flies whole across its crest.
Even the knot holes
in the tree trunk

sing out to the wings
—this according
to Burchfield's

brush. A swift
black line
of tar

mends cracks
in the pavement.
A stroke

shifting back
and forth, a curve
determined by the fault

that precedes it.
The trace of a tree
in the road—

beautiful black
on black: wild
branches,

gangling
vines;
and I imagine:

Burchfield Brothers and Co.
Tar artists, road
show workers going down

the street with their boiling pitch,
as if caulking
the hull of our leaky ship.

What are you drawing?
Just lines.
It's nothing? . . . Maybe it's

trees
or people. From whole
to whole—

the landscape as entire tree,
the *inscape*. "Reasoning is
a simple divination"

—John Henry might
have written that for
his friend Gerard Hopkins.

The tree boughs
bent together as
a doorframe, or

the ivy crown
wreathed and worn for
a like opening:

the mind's rising music.
I divine from what's under the sun
the poem's first cause.

THE **GEE'S BEND** QUILTERS / THE **MUSEUM** OF **MODERN ART**

Kandinsky saw the quilts at Gee's Bend
in a vision: a tree breaking
into a hundred green notes
dotting brown corduroy.

Mondrian had his own vision:
blocked out boogie woogie rhythms
shocked across gray in
syncopated pink

and Motherwell saw prison stripes
over faded mottled strips
of blue jeans—wet paint played
under loose cut paper.

Motherwell, most of all,
must have seen them:
the way a Mediterranean wash
can shimmer by the power

of one gold bolt,
off side, trembling fast.
Wrinkled red and blue *Open
Summer*. God is saying something

about the way awkwardness stumbles
into beauty, but keeps
its awkwardness
as a grace. The way

a hand is young
when it is very old
and knows
the tatters as

whole cloth. God
lets us
fall into what cuts
across time, to keep us.

Pale blue-gray
ovoid knee patches
from every bent day—
now a cloudy hierarchy.

Essie Bendolph Pettway,
you know it better than O'Keeffe;
you take the order to its origin on your knees
(those seams are fine white cotton rows).

Black bars lead inexorably into free
infinity—
Loretta Pettway, you know it better
than Anselm Kiefer,

for your family was first
taken by the hand
and led
where they did not want to go.

Irene Williams, you know
as well as Franz Kline
what an iron dark girder will do
to a humid sky.

Lorraine Pettway
Latisha Pettway
Pearlie Pettway
Missouri Pettway,

you take the critic past his head
and put him, poor, by a bend
in the river, in the mud
by a hissing silver maple.

Let these rhapsodies
sew up
the rhetoric of *high* and *low*.
Michelangelo,

I saw the dove descend in Alabama.

GEORGES ROUAULT / ROBERT **MOTHERWELL**

The face, the refrain
of the face. Francis Bacon
gave us

an igneous
or metamorphic
metaphor:

the eyes
boil up, the mouth
smears

under heat and pressure.
In the geologic
history of painting,

the shifting of split
face planes precedes
the molten muse,

but in whichever
of these recent rooms,
gravity

shall not
assuage us
with its flat

averages.
What is known,
what still desired,

in the stone grown
equanimity
of a lichen gray eye?

If I am going
to seek (again)
the first face,

past our broken
and hallowed
critique,

I would rather follow
Rouault's finger-
thick black outlines,

hard as carbon on a cave wall,
something older than medieval
iconography, returning to

what it returned to
—a logos of color and line
risen to the surface

of dark flood water—
Veronica's veil
across the face of the deep.

Barnacled pain:
the black lines
are encrusted blood.

More than a trace:
a topographic map
of the whole human face

where modernism
is one drop of sweat.
Where do the black pools

in Motherwell's heavy *Elegies*
come from?
Great canting shapes,

bars and biomorphs:
slow notes leaning
one upon another

in Górecki's third symphony,
or the enormous tragedy
in the peasant's bent

shoulders Pound witnessed
in Pisa. No smearing
of the tragedy. No closing

of the eyes that go
right to the center of sight,
accusing and forgiving

in one clear look.
Perspective's
brittle lines

shatter; Bacon's makeshift
rooms collapse,
while communal

grief remains
open, fluid. Rouault's rivers
feed into Mother-

well's blood. It must be offered up,
past its weight,
back to the human face.

MARTIN **HEIDEGGER** / **EZRA** POUND
(AN ENIGMA LIES A PRIORI IN EVERY RELATION)

Pale green buffalo grass,
soft, moves off
to the lawn's lean jetty that edges
the parking lot—

far nub lit up with lupin,
standing purple for three feet—
color, before the searing heat
takes it down in late June.

And now it is late July. Heidegger,
the question of being has been cut
with the being of the question
for nearly a century. The question

jetties from its continental
body, out to the isolate
dot of leftover dried purple.
Who thinks, who cares

who thinks, who dares
—from the stereo: cyclic
lyric spun to one self-
searcher: *dasein*. The front man

in the heavy metal band
runs along the jetty from the stage
out into the audience. On his earphone
he can hear guitar, bass, and drums

balanced with his voice. He sings
at the center of incredible volume
of which he is a part: one with an audience
to his own voice. He is wireless,

without connection, out in the middle
of five thousand darkened faces—the pure roar
of relentless ocean. Enigma
and light trade places—the beam

over surging waves. What gleams
in the metal posture? How fast
it all
becomes reflex.

We have done our best;
we have come
close as we can
to severing being

from meaning, seemingly
unaware that once
the tendon is cut,
both are lost to us.

The pierced word rises through the roar—
the piercing question—*the undistorted*
presencing of the thing
in wind of an unknown source. Sound

goes past the probing edge, the specially
constructed stage
whose meaning is exhausted
in constructed charisma.

What is this goes past the voice.
What juts through—
an irruption as from
the audible ground

as if the apex of volume
gave birth to its other side. The far off
front man's purple shirt
waves in and out of hot light. His voice lost

in a stillness that reclaims us
even while the solo sears us.
Alethia: revealingness.
From the mass

of sound, some missa. *Alethia:*
a flower's name
when opening.
As if from the surge

of the irrational
we might reach
"A Station of the Metro." These faces,
these faces, and the beauty

of the ringing night. The afterlight
of the question: why do we see
past dried up sight?
A moon in the sum of it,

or past that too,
a beginningless beginning (we can still
make it new). A far nub of thought
where late headlights turn over lupin.

OSCAR **MUÑOZ** / EMMANUEL **LEVINAS**
(AFTER TWO PIECES BY MUÑOZ AT SITE SANTA FE)

1

The artist tries to paint his self portrait
with water
on concrete that darkens with each

quick stroke. Here
the suggestion of an eye,
there a mouth. Now

a slight shadow under the chin,
but the eye has already faded
and the eyebrow evaporates.

He is painting the forehead,
and now the line of a cheek,
but the chin is gone;

the mouth for a moment holds
and the right eye again is shaped
while the left one disappears . . .

The hand's
alacrity
is exhausted by its efforts

while the face remains,
"its own
invocation."

In whose eyes
will you see it again?
"Completely naked,

the face signifies
itself—" breath beneath
the very skin of the sign,

a circle sign and yet
a well uncircumscribed, fading
in the water that would figure it.

Love, the other
is complete
in your incompletion,

in water and breath,
in failure. "I am never finished
with emptying myself of myself."

2

Levinas,
it is you who leans
over and steams

the wide steel paten
where the face
lies hidden

in a sheen
of grease.
Your word

lifts it
into life. Here
from the shallows

of each mirror
men and women
come to focus

by virtue
of your breath. Muñoz,
his breath in yours

where emptying
is most full. An arc of intent
from one end of the body

to the other
where pain itself is a light,
a link, a Lear-like

tenderness:
"Lend me a looking glass,
if that her breath will mist

or stain the stone,
why,
then she lives."

O that sight
might take
its measure

from these
respirations—
whispered portraits.

KARL **RAHNER** /
THE **DUSKY SEASIDE** SPARROW
(FOR ALEXIS PALMAFFY)

Tweezers to put the rigging up—
filament buoyed by light—
masts like the bones of the smallest bird

erected under glass.
These dexterous threads—
spun from attention that cannot tremble.

From glass to breath—there is no ocean
can bring this ship improved
to a substantial shore.

There is no improvement
can spark substance. The message dead
in this bottle, and yet the message

still, is read: *Dusky—"Orange"*
—Last one
Died 16 June 87

tagged to the lid.
How could there be zero
for the dusky seaside sparrow?

Shall these bones not also sing
of the full form they were
and could be? An ounce,

perhaps,
flying back, reified
from where? We cannot conceive

how it could not be.
It is not an issue
of science; it is an issue

of love coextensive with the world.
The bottled bird carcass
cannot possibly focus the hope

behind it. Dark feathers matted
in the preservative liquid, its eyes
cataract white.

That we would think this way *at all*
as Karl Rahner would say.
Where death drops like a pebble

the smallest bird,
the rings of its imagined flight
circle and grow in *nous poietikos*.

That we would think this way at all—
predilections
of agent intellect—

every terminus
in a wider
horizon of *yes*

where breath
draws form. The horizon exceeds us,
or rather (to go with Rahner)

takes us with it,
holding the sky-
blue hem (*who*

touched me,
just then?) Something small
worthy of eternity

fits perfectly
the *Proem* of the world.
Nous poietikos

skylights the deep
searching for the leaf
to focus hope. The hummingbird

in my hallway
beat against the window, pitched
pleading, frantic under glass, finally

stayed poised on the broom handle
while I carried it outside.
It has gone for the world

from what's whole to a caged
inanition, the spell unspoken,
caught in the bottle, but to go

for once, from what's broken
to what's whole, this is
the lasting marriage, or more

this is
kenosis equal to creation—
feather flutter in the trembling water.

The ship in the corked bottle
is light as a message
and would float,

but what kind of message—
to send a paper sail,
a model of escape,

not a mode but a model,
bowed blank white
surrender I send myself

these years on the booked-up shore.
Once I went in sleep
from hospital

helicopter to humming
bird moth: kingdom
broacher, who at evening

was the mollifying
magic between
the sunset colored hollyhocks

and what lies behind all sunsets
that is not composed of darkness.
Far humming thing,

you carried a man half dead.
Let each inscrutable *no*
be overshadowed by another

pulse, another measure. Even in death
prepared to pierce
the nectared darkness: *vorgriff*,

that great
Rahner word;
what bird flies through it

nor hawk nor eagle,
but something dusky small
we guess dead. *Vorgriff*

its grinding consonant
makes a rift
in an iron heavy cliff

so that the night shows
through the beak-like opening.
Alexis Palmaffy told me—

down the long hallway
of this poem—
she pulled free a tiny bird-

wing from the flypaper.
With the wing
splayed back, the bird turned

to look at her. I carry
that same creature now,
down the same hallway,

crouched over
its thin cry—
bird yet

to be born. Each creature
marks another horizon,
a flight past sight's extinction.

We know a little vision
sinewed with temerity
that in each of us is maybe

worthy of eternity.
The dusky seaside sparrow
darts in the eyes of an old woman

waiting at the Greyhound station.
She can barely get up, she soars
through something already gone.

THOMAS AQUINAS / EMILY DICKINSON

1

His apophatic fog-
hat comes off

for the shine
of her oil-stain rainbow.

2

"It's all straw"

"I wish I were a hay"

JOAN MITCHELL / CHARLES OLSON

A complex gestural nest:
burnt orange and flame-yellow
mixed with pooling green and pale flaked blue.

Do these unplatonic colors, impure,
holding reign as by default,
cry down into the unprimed canvas

a place as for some birth unpainted,
unknown—an empty nest holding claim
on us, a place in us we fill and fail to fill?

        Williams saw a bundle below the bridge
        in Juarez.

        An inhuman shapelessness,
        a sack of rags,

    and yet
        Egg shaped!

> Something that completes
> the circuit of the *Desert Music;*

> something unexpected in the excavation.

The veins go on, stained with gravity. There may be
another nest below us; one birth
under another, one birth

through another. Each nest
an arc of intent for the next. How is it in this mess
of pigment, color's praxis seems intact?

> As Olson puts it in *The Kingfishers,*

>> *this nest of excrement and decayed fish*
>> *becomes a dripping fetid mass*

> for the birth of the bird whose breast
> bears the color of the sun.

A humble height: Duncan who looked down
into Olson's excavation site,

    seemed also to look up:
    A worm

    or a reflection of a star
    moved in the depths.
    A star may be a crawling thing.

Or, as he says elsewhere: a salamander, a
    fairie of the fire,
    the radiant crawling.

Welling in the worm holes of nest upon nest,
but rising as by color's first call, the denouement
of the necessary tangle, the painting raining

down into the deeps of its mind,
while maintaining
these fiery saturations at the top.

In the *nest's muck,*
among rocks,
in the egg-shaped bundle of rags,

color itself is transfigured.

ROBERT **DUNCAN** / **DANTE** ALIGHIERI

"They all posited an infinite
first principal
as though compelled by truth itself,
yet they did not recognize their own voice."

Their own voice
got in the way. "We
pretend to speak. The language
is not ours

and we move upward beyond
our powers into
words again
beyond us, unsure measures."

So poetry notes
its own crumbling
and yet behind it shines
the prime

Proem. Theos
comes from *theaste*
(to consider, to see)
—this according to Aquinas.

By *Ground Work* Duncan
wanted very much a
falling-into-seeing that sought
the end.

"A million reapers come to cut down
the leaves of grass we hoped to live by
except we give ourselves utterly over to the
end of things."

In the end then, if we give in,
the good of the whole
is recovered, a given whole that contains
its losses and evolutions,

and yet the self
that Whitman sought
seems no longer to suffice.
Now it is "the country way

incapable of speech
driven toward impending speech."
What voice did he want
of the end of things?

And what precedes
such speaking in the flame of eschatology?
"Long time ago I knew and came
to a knowledge of the bitter core of me,

the clinker soul, the stubborn residue
that needed the fire and refused to burn."
If I were Dante I'd place Duncan with Statius
talking and talking, a circling man,

on the narrow rise
all the way to the fire. He might talk
of the lady he addresses
in his *Metaphysical Suite:*

"My nature I knew not
in her, who held the questioning key
that would unlock in full the answering
male Moon."

—wanting an answer in full to his nature,
the blank in the mirror before its shattering,
the beginnings of poetry . . .
and the end?

"Restore my conscience to its first command"
—is that Duncan or Saint Paul?
It is a call from whom, from where? Perhaps
the parting words with Statius, or even Dante.

(It is in the Thebaid's *asides*
where Dante listens to Statius:
"My task is to give length to lives"
—the poet as lover not destroyer.)

Restore
my conscience to its first
command:
anamesis in a timeless place.

"*Our father Who Art in Heaven* . . . I begin
my prayer before the Night, and, gazing in,
I wonder at the depth that I call *Him*."
The Him or Hymn of an opening-convergence.

The poem is always all quotes,
the whirling of a thousand voices from a poet who was not afraid
to call himself derivative and dilettante.
"—the stirring of that Harp of Spheres or vaster

music of Saints or Stars whirling in the ecstatic Rose. . . ." In this
I become his voice and his becomes mine.
I am conduced to a vision
where sight arises from its pyre.

FRANCIS / **CLARE**

     Write
     the
WHITE *letters*
     on
     a
     Paschal **OATH**
     candle

Clare, her
hair cut. Fair
fallen to make fair,
brown-blond to the floor for

Lady Poverty and
a better grace than that
worn for glory.
Clare, her

bare feet stepping clear
from the scattered curls.
My Clare at
Santa Maria de la Paz—her

coffee brown eyes that go on and on into
a pool of innocence upon whose shore

we both can stand.
My Clare, I

speak to you across such waters as you carry.
My Lady and
my lady—
these white

divisions.
Shall I tell you
apart?
I tell you:

from start to
finish, my
life needs
forgiveness.

"He my peace /
my parting,
sword and strife"
I read Hopkins

and think of Clare.
How he knows

the sonnet's line must go
to its end and yet

must break
precisely where
peace abrogates
from other loves.

His slash mark
the sword stroke.
—A poetics
harshly driven

of Ecclesia:

                Vertical
                horizons
                sear
INCAN-   *sentences*
                each
                line   **DESCENT**
                claimed

A poetics
harshly driven, and yet

isn't Ecclesia
all voices

commingling;
and that pool, *her*
pool, "the company
of love"?

                    Shall
                    the
                    mind
                    be
MIRROR   *clear*
                    of
                    aching   **MOUTH**
                    horizons?

MARC CHAGALL / ALEXIS PALMAFFY

1

What Color is Paradise?
—a children's book
on Marc Chagall.

He never learned
how to paint inside
the outlines:

a burst of yellow
that half covers
a fish—flash

of color come loose.
A green tree
wreathed with flame

under purple water
(going one up
on Moses).

Who can call
the colors home
to their idea:

they leap away,
breathing the free meaning's
respiration.

2

Alexis Palmaffy draws
a string tied to the finger,
then loops it down
into a stork's satchel,

so memory gives birth
but first needs to be carried
asleep, hands curled in
a deeper fold of world.

Marc in his red coat:
so joyful a young man
(perhaps a little drunk)

riding on the shoulders of his new wife
Bella: strong and beautiful
in her white dress.

How lovely he paints himself
carried by her
as Dante by Lucia:

"Then she and my sleep went away at once."

So quickly, so quickly

Bella dead and Marc
turned all his paintings
to face the wall.

3

Alexis, I look
at your Bella
whose body

is torqued to become
the star she reaches for.
The white light

around her hand,
a clearing in the etching.

Memory burned
into *anamesis*
where we can look

straight at the star's
fine-tined filament.

4

How do you know
the name of the sun?

I know it from
number upon number
spun therefrom. (The code in the flower
is not prose.)

Joy could not for long
be turned toward the wall.

Marc and Alexis,
joy your leit-
motif for larger
life, where animals

are always with us
turning from the great pinwheeled sun

into the world;
arms thrown out drunkenly,
on the shoulders of the one you love.

5

Who can bring
the colors in;

they play out
over their creatures

as if color
encreatured itself;

the joy form
manifest, blest
in flesh and blood.

Come at Easter,
pinwheeled from my need.

6

My friend told me about her father:

In his last week of life, he said
that each night a beautiful
woman would come to him, and sit

at his bedside,
and at the moment
he woke, she would be gone.

And he said: *I just don't know
how much longer
I will be able to resist her.*

MOTHER / SON

I've seen him several times
crossing my small town,
up Central down Trinity,
along Diamond where it goes

into the pines. He may live
in the concrete caves
called Little Mexico—
the undocumented stay there

in big families. I notice him
because he always wears
the same tee shirt, the one with flames
over the Sacred Heart. Get close

and the flames are like a crown.
This town, per capita,
has the most Ph.D.s in the United States.
The Atomic City

the official tee shirt says
below the cartoon glow
of the mushroom cloud.
I like to think of him, a kid

on his way to one job or another,
carrying the heart
and the flames
back and forth.

—The trace of a public
signal grace, a
candling in common threads.
"We are not judged

but by a direction,"
wrote Oppen,
or by a vision:
love in the utterly

pragmatic:
"When did we
see you Lord?"
Just work, confirmed by the feet.

In the hospital
a private sign—
his crossing
drawn to *her* point—

the icon in the x-ray:
image
of the Guadalupe
Virgin

 above her breast
(the medal left
around her neck).
A brand

across the cancer,
our Lady's
imprimatur
over the heart.

"We are close enough to childhood,
so easily purged"
of whatever this world
thought we were to be.

Come, and you can find
these two
loves meeting.
Let these two

graces
signal
each other:
walking in the image,

resting in the image.
Plurally present,
the flame-drawn
signature.

SAINT FAUSTINA / KAROL WOJTYLA

The face
the refrain
of the face.
Saint Faustina

and her vision
of red rays from the right side
of the sacred heart, white
rays from the left.

Together, they are a kind
of Ab-Ex triangle:
flying lines
of fire and water.

Above them
the familiar face—
perhaps the least abstract
of anything we know.

Faustina wanted
the body and blood
translated into a pure grace
of light,

painted,
and yet she knew
that no image
would do the vision justice.

R
  a
    c
      i
        n
          g   quiet eyes
        l
      i
    g
  h
t

It was an art action
when Karol Wojtyla
processed through the streets
of communist Krakow

with an empty frame
that once held
an icon
of the Mother of God.

The streets full
of worshipers;
everyone knew
what the missing image was.

It was
by holy imagination
not really missing.
Who's to say

the image was not in some way
more perfectly venerated,
presented so silently and then
submerged again in every heart.

From the passion back
to all of us.
Even the transfigured body
in a sacred blaze, contains

its labor, a
circumscription
of sacrifice
breathed back.

At five o'clock, light
from the stained glass window
fills the Faustina
icon: a red

inundation,
taking
all the image save
the halo.

ENIGMA AND **LIGHT** IN EVERY **RELATION** I

1

> *I found myself inside a prayer*
> *by praying it, and there*
> *were many men and women,*
> *ancient faces, not old*
>
> *in years, but as*
> *first peoples, eyes clear,*
> *seeing in full fierce*
> *innocence.*

The midst of the furnace like a moist whistling wind
where Shadrach, Meshach, and Abednego
walk
        praising God.

A figure beside them, four, one other,
a figure of water through fire.

Praise here the key. Praise
opens a chord in the beatific vision
where notes or elements drop or rise
according to the need's accompaniment.

A string theory
of spun dimensions. A sapient
concatenation:
language braided with creation.

As the *Book of Wisdom* puts it:

> "For the elements changed places with one another
> as on a harp the notes vary the nature of the rhythm,
> while each note remains the same."

Elements like notes move to a different string
yet sound as they were,
so fire passes through water
and yet is fire; and a man

might pass through fire unhurt,
praising for the passage—
the notes of fire played on a scale
above or below him.

> *Our Father who art in Heaven . . .*

> *I begin my prayer on earth before the night,*
> *listening until I am the word earth*

moving swift across the line
toward their kingdom cries

Pound's *Unwobbling Pivot:* "A man
standing by his word,"
a breathing ideogram,
with its centered spear shaft

—the vortex of imagism
"from which and through which and
into which ideas are constantly rushing."
A radiant gist   *an image of God*

in the midst of the furnace.
The midst of the furnace like a moist
whistling wind,   a vortex through which
the Spirit passes, an

angelic ideogram
singing in the wind tunnel,
in holy Meta-
        metaphor, across the margins of the scale.

2

In *Daniel* we read: "The fingers of a man's hand
appeared, and wrote on the plaster wall
of the king's palace, opposite the lampstand,
and the king saw the hand as it wrote."

Fingers of flame writing
the names of eastern measures;
and the prophet in alliterative divination
links the burning verbs:

Mina: manah: to measure
(God has numbered your days).
Shekel: saqal: to weigh
(you have been weighed in the balance

and found wanting). It is I
so weighed and measured,
found lacking praxis born of faith.
My own wall is written on:

*From the streetlight
outside my window,
winter and*

*an arrow—
a white line drawn
from a slit in the Venetian blinds*

*across the corner and behind
the bookshelf, stops
precisely at*

*the crucifix,
as if I had known
to nail it there.*

*I get up to investigate: the line
drops sharply,
rises*

*in a V, runs
across the Rothko print,
(the back side*

of God
that Moses saw) claims
its numinosity.

Night after night
from the blinds,
how the light

lifts and ends
fed into the
left arm of the cross.

Missa: *to be sent,*
to be pierced,
by something within . . .

by something . . .
I am not thinking
of Saint Teresa

and her Renaissance Cupid,
and yet the figures of this signal grace
sharpen with need.

What numinosity, claimed or negated
near the lampstand in a paltry or a royal room.
Negated to be claimed. "Every apohaptic sentence is in a sense
'haunted' by God." Scottus Eriugena's

cataphatic backmasking: the *Proem* at the end
of the pistil. Creation's pen
writing the icon of Creator. A cursive creaturehood
bright with theophany—propinquity in blue
and gold flowing lines.

3

How did you learn
the name of the sun?
I learned it from
the sun himself.

The signature so ardent
it seems almost enough
to burn the canvas—

the name become
the whole image. O in o
or winnowed
o in O (so

John Scottus shows me). "God allows creation to be responsible
for his own unfolding name."
I am the word earth burning across the line
    toward their kingdom cries.

Praise arcs where first is final cause.
Praise bends the note in an arc of need.
Praise pierces. Praise the opening-
    convergence.

Praise makes a place where breath tents the pray-er.
Praise the inherent similarity in dissimilars
inceptive to the *Proem* of the Cosmos.
Praise the Always More

A pentecost lies coiled in these relations
a spiral jetty
across the sweet salt water of the mind.

The exemplar: a radiant
arc of intent   in the first furnace.
Light streams across the bowl of the valley
into the high horizon's peak.

I found myself inside a prayer . . .

ENIGMA AND **LIGHT** IN EVERY **RELATION** II

1

The priest focuses on the crucifix at the far end of the church
that no one else can see;
everyone else looks at the one above and behind the altar, a crucifix
the priest, as he consecrates, can't see.

> *Wound sees wound,*
> *sees you   sees me*

Every instrument, every
song, begins from some
kind of hollow: the puckered

whistle or the bellowed cry,
the singing cavern clarifying
emptiness. What is the soul

but a whisper
whirled into form
that knows itself by the matter

of its tramping song
by night. By night
one need leads to another.

In the etching by Alexis Palmaffy,
the hole in the head
echoes the hole in the galaxy

above it,
both with spiral
fracture lines.

I feel thy finger and find thee
touching the flute hole in my head,
the worm hole in my heart,

God shaped,
that riffs itself, coiling
into the music of some other sphere.

Come at Christmas,
come at Easter,
pinwheeled to and from my need.

2

Today's pedestrian phylacteries:
        iPods fastened to the arm.

In my head in-
culcated celerity: virtual
fingers flying
toward the siren of the hard drive.

Who can hear the human through the "mu-
sic," as Olson calls it in *Maximus*
—the sick muse bound to us . . .

> *shhh   shhh*
> *of the wide-bristled broom*
> *against the stone floor*

The telos of any art: to fructify the human
(there is no art in the *Inferno*).

Bending, they saw the carved images in the stone floor,
exemplum of humility, in bas-relief—
tooled and smoothed waves of muscle and linen.

(I stroke his shoulders and his face
when I clean the stations
in the main church.)

Creation is by nature bas-relief, its moving communications
half in, half out
        of the substratum.

(Hope is a kind of bas-relief.)

        shhh   shhh
            clean to see
    shapes in the shine near the altar

The fold in the hills
still holds the road,

and yet it is another holding
back of me,
a wealth reflected forth
I cannot reach by reaching.

"We know that we are cleansed
when the will itself
surprises the soul with the freedom to change."

—rhymes with Paradise: "I would marvel if,
free from impediment, you had remained below.
Like fire you ought to rise."

      shhh   shhh
          under the votive light

Recessed into the wall
the lamp so deep you see the tines

of its filament glow distinct—
orange through the thick-
bellied yellow glass—

a tuning fork for another music
unheard yet, the tines
fine as hairs, burning hot, numbered
three, immolated yet remaining.

Unheard yet, this music that is light
and yet it is anterior to all
orchestral caverns

      shhh   shhh
          flame in stillness rising

3

    Music half in half out
        of the substratum.

    Leonard Bernstein lifted his face
    into the final measure
    of the last symphony
    he conducted—

    exultant, beatific, percipient
    even, transcending sex,
    transcending everything,
    holding that moment.

    —The first measures of a symphony
    counted out in silence
    over and again.

NOTES

Poems in this book make use of brief lines and phrases from the following works: *The Making of Americans* by Gertrude Stein; the poems of Robert Creeley, Robert Duncan, Gerard Manley Hopkins, Charles Olson, and William Carlos Williams; and *Summa Contra Gentiles* by Thomas Aquinas. The reference in the first line of "Mark Chagall / Alexis Palmaffy" comes from Elisabeth Lemke, whose book is titled *What Color Is Paradise?*

ABOUT THE AUTHOR

DAVID MUTSCHLECNER is the author of *Sign* (2007) and *Esse* (2002), both from Ahsahta Press, and *Veils*, from Stride (UK).

AHSAHTA PRESS

SAWTOOTH POETRY PRIZE SERIES

2002: Aaron McCollough, *Welkin* (Brenda Hillman, judge)
2003: Graham Foust, *Leave the Room to Itself* (Joe Wenderoth, judge)
2004: Noah Eli Gordon, *The Area of Sound Called the Subtone* (Claudia Rankine, judge)
2005: Karla Kelsey, *Knowledge, Forms, The Aviary* (Carolyn Forché, judge)
2006: Paige Ackerson-Kiely, *In No One's Land* (D. A. Powell, judge)
2007: Rusty Morrison, *the true keeps calm biding its story* (Peter Gizzi, judge)
2008: Barbara Maloutas, *the whole Marie* (C. D. Wright, judge)
2009: Julie Carr, *100 Notes on Violence* (Rae Armantrout, judge)
2010: James Meetze, *Dayglo* (Terrance Hayes, judge)
2011: Karen Rigby, *Chinoiserie* (Paul Hoover, judge)

AHSAHTA PRESS

NEW SERIES

1. Lance Phillips, *Corpus Socius*
2. Heather Sellers, *Drinking Girls and Their Dresses*
3. Lisa Fishman, *Dear, Read*
4. Peggy Hamilton, *Forbidden City*
5. Dan Beachy-Quick, *Spell*
6. Liz Waldner, *Saving the Appearances*
7. Charles O. Hartman, *Island*
8. Lance Phillips, *Cur aliquid vidi*
9. Sandra Miller, *oriflamme.*
10. Brigitte Byrd, *Fence Above the Sea*
11. Ethan Paquin, *The Violence*
12. Ed Allen, *67 Mixed Messages*
13. Brian Henry, *Quarantine*
14. Kate Greenstreet, *case sensitive*
15. Aaron McCollough, *Little Ease*
16. Susan Tichy, *Bone Pagoda*
17. Susan Briante, *Pioneers in the Study of Motion*
18. Lisa Fishman, *The Happiness Experiment*
19. Heidi Lynn Staples, *Dog Girl*
20. David Mutschlecner, *Sign*
21. Kristi Maxwell, *Realm Sixty-four*
22. G. E. Patterson, *To and From*
23. Chris Vitiello, *Irresponsibility*
24. Stephanie Strickland, *Zone : Zero*
25. Charles O. Hartman, *New and Selected Poems*
26. Kathleen Jesme, *The Plum-Stone Game*
27. Ben Doller, *FAQ:*
28. Carrie Olivia Adams, *Intervening Absence*
29. Rachel Loden, *Dick of the Dead*
30. Brigitte Byrd, *Song of a Living Room*
31. Kate Greenstreet, *The Last 4 Things*
32. Brenda Iijima, *If Not Metamorphic*
33. Sandra Doller, *Chora.*
34. Susan Tichy, *Gallowglass*
35. Lance Phillips, *These Indicium Tales*
36. Karla Kelsey, *Iteration Nets*
37. Brian Teare, *Pleasure*
38. Kristen Kaschock, *A Beautiful Name for a Girl*
39. Susan Briante, *Utopia Minus*
40. Brian Henry, *Lessness*
41. Lisa Fishman, *FLOWER CART*
42. Aaron McCollough, *No Grave Can Hold My Body Down*
43. Kristi Maxwell, *Re-*
44. Andrew Grace, *Sancta*
45. Chris Vitiello, *Obedience*
46. Paige Ackerson-Kiely, *My Love Is a Dead Arctic Explorer*
47. David Mutschlecner, *Enigma and Light*

This book is set in Apollo MT type
with DIN Light and Bold titles
by Ahsahta Press at Boise State University.
Cover design by Quemadura.
Book design by Janet Holmes.
Printed in Canada.

AHSAHTA PRESS

2012

JANET HOLMES, DIRECTOR
JODI CHILSON, MANAGING EDITOR

KYLE CRAWFORD   JESSICA JOHNSON, *intern*
CHARLES GABEL   GENNA KOHLHARDT
KATE HOLLAND   JULIE STRAND
WALLY HUMPHRIES   JASON STEPHENS, *intern*
TORIN JENSEN   MATT TRUSLOW
ZACH VESPER